To Jony,
my pal and
reepmate,
with deep
appreciation,
Jerry

ORIGINAL RIDDLES
AND
SATIRICAL FABLES GALORE

By Gerald Amada

ORIGINAL RIDDLES
AND
SATIRICAL FABLES GALORE
First Edition

Published by:
Biographical Publishing Company
95 Sycamore Drive
Prospect, CT 06712-1493
Phone: 203-758-3661
Fax: 253-793-2618
e-mail: biopub@aol.com

PRINTED IN THE UNITED STATES OF AMERICA

Publisher's Cataloging-in-Publication Data
Amada, Gerald
Original Riddles and Satirical Fables Galore / by Gerald Amada.
1st ed.
p. cm.
ISBN 1736901915 (alk. Paper)
13-Digit ISBN 9781736901915
1. Title. 2. Humor. 3. Riddles 4. Fables.
Dewey Decimal Classification: 817 American Wit and Humor
BISAC Subject:
    HUM004000 HUMOR / Form / Jokes & Riddles
    HUM018000 HUMOR / Form / Puns & Wordplay
Library of Congress Control Number: 2021921547

This book is dedicated to my son, Eric Amada and my
grandson, Joshua Tzucker
With love and deep appreciation

Question: What is the difference between a puddle and a poodle?

Answer: A puddle is a small pool of water. A poodle is a dog. Furthermore, puddles can often be found in many homes, often directly beneath a poodle.

Question: What has been the fastest growing mountain in the United States?

Answer: Mt. Rushmore, of course.

Question: What do you call a violinist who constantly tells riddles?

Answer: A riddling fiddler or, if you prefer, a fiddling riddler.

Question: What is the difference between a mailman and a merman?

Answer: A mailman is sometimes drenched while delivering mail in a storm. A merman is always drenched when thwacking his tail to deliver maelstroms.

Question: What happens when models pose for too many cheesecake photographs?

Answer: They gain excessive weight, cease to be models and join Weight Watchers, anonymously.

Question: What do a bagel and a synagogue have in common?

Answer: A bagel is holey after it has been boiled and baked and a synagogue is a religious institution, a holy citadel of the Jewish faith, that should not, however, be eaten under any circumstances. Both are wholly Jewish in nature but only one of them is religious and the other goes quite well with cream cheese and lox when served at a celebration immediately after a synagogue's Bar Mitzvah services.

Question: What song is sung at the opening of conventions attended largely by optometrists?

Answer: The National Anthem, of course. Why, might you ask? Because it begins with the words, "Oh, say can you see….?"

Question: What is the difference between a golf club and a Golf Club.

Answer: A golf club is a club used to hit a golf ball in a game of golf. A Golf Club is an aggregate of members who pay hefty dues for the perverse pleasure of shanking golf balls into bushes and deriving an even deeper gratification from informing their friends and relatives that they spend a great deal of time and money indulging themselves by golfing in this kind of classy setting.

Question: What is the difference between a clamshell and a clam's hell?

Answer: A clamshell is the shell of a clam, formed of two roughly equal valves with a hinge. A clam's hell is when the clam finds itself on the menu of a seafood restaurant.

Question: What should you do when you come to a fork in the road?

Answer: A farmhand of my acquaintance strolled away from his job to venture upon a farm road with which he was unfamiliar. After a few miles of casual sightseeing, he came upon a fork in the road. He was transfixed by this fork, which glistened up into his eyes, reflecting a very bright ray of sunlight. He bent down and picked up this solitary fork, inspected it carefully, and realized that there was a special elegance beneath the grime and oil it had accumulated for many months or years.

He took the fork back to the farm and scrubbed it into a state of glistening stature. He placed the fork in his traveling case, intending to keep it as an inseparable friend. A few days later he returned to the road where he had come upon the fork. Instead of the fork he was, alas, to find a dork in the road. The dork was leaning against a post, crying hysterically. My friend reached out to him with concern by asking him the cause of his misery. In response, the dork said he had purchased from a farmer several chickens a few weeks ago. He purchased the chickens so he might have a regular supply of eggs to meet his dietary needs. After several weeks there were no eggs, leaving him feeling cheated and distraught. My friend asked him if the cages he had set upon the road contained the chickens. He said that they were the very same ones. My friend approached the cages, peered in and made a startling discovery: the four chickens were roosters!

My friend didn't bother to break the bad news to the dork. He sadly left him sobbing on the road and returned to the farmhouse. That night, he left with the fork.

Now, as for the matter of what to do when you encounter a fork in the road, I'd suggest that you wrap it up in a paper towel, take it home, give it a soapy bath and then decide whether you wish to employ it as a utensil or, instead, take it out as a companion to an elegant restaurant for dinner, using the restaurant's tableware to eat your meal.

As for dealing with dorks on the road or elsewhere, I think it's best not to panic and, if necessary, try to pretend you're deaf or don't speak their language.

Question: What do you call drunken workers who plaster walls?

Answer: Plastered plasterers.

Question: What did the gefilte fish say when it had been gruffly shoved into the far corner of the dinner table by the chopped liver?

Answer: "What do you think I am, chopped liver, like you?"

Question: What do you call the person who delivers screws to hardware stores?

Answer: A screwdriver, of course.

Question: Why does practically everyone brush their teeth?

Answer: Because it's much easier than brushing someone else's teeth.

Question: Why do most people carry a handkerchief or Kleenex with them?

Answer: Obviously, it's to blow or sneeze into either one with your nostrils. Naturally, one must realize that blowing or sneezing with one's own nose is far easier and tidier than blowing or sneezing by enlisting another person's nose for this purpose.

Question: Why has Santa Claus particularly entrusted reindeer to pull his sleigh these many years?

Answer: A learned authority on this subject has informed me of the true history of Santa's escapades, highlighting, of course, Santa's heedless affinity for sooty chimneys. When Santa was a young, beardless man, he lacked ambition and the requisite skills to qualify for gainful employment. Thus, he went to see his grandfather, who was regarded as a font of wisdom throughout their village. His grandfather, a wealthy but very charitable man, noted Santa's acute need for delivery boys who could deliver gifts to needful children during the Christmas holidays. He purchased for Santa, at considerable expense, a large bevy of miniature poodles which he hitched to a sleigh laden with weighty Christmas gifts for his grandson Santa to commandeer on his nightly forays into the dark and distant firmament.

Well, within three days the poodles were, quite predictably, horribly exhausted and demoralized by their nightly flights. Irate, they complained to Santa and threatened to quit. Santa, a self-righteous man, rebuffed their complaints and fired them. When his grandfather, who happened to be the village mayor at that time, learned of this crisis, he purchased eight reindeer from a farmer and gave them to his grandson, Santa. A lawyer, representing the poodles, took the matter to court, claiming an injustice had been perpetrated. As mayor, Santa's grandfather defended his grandson, claiming broad privileges as the original owner of the poodles. After three days of legalistic haggling in the courtroom, Santa's argument, based on original ownership, prevailed. The argument attracted widespread attention throughout the legal profession and henceforth became a widely invoked legal principle known as – wouldn't you know it? – a Grandfather Claus, named of course for its eponym, the rich owner of the poodles. Due to a regrettable lexical mistake that took place about two hundred years later, the letter "e" was added to the name Claus and the legal phrase was "decapitalized." Because of this inept mistake the public has henceforth been misled into believing grievous falsehoods about Santa Claus and his eight reindeer rather than the true history of Santa and his fourteen downtrodden miniature poodles, as it is depicted in the authentic narrative you have just read.

Question: What is the difference between carrots and carats?

Answer: Carrots are a biennial herb with an orange spindle. Carrots keep blood sugar levels down and they're loaded with vitamin A and beta carotene, which potentially can lower a person's diabetic risk. Moreover, the calcium and vitamin K in carrots are important for bone health. In other words, if you find the time and inclination to eat carrots, they can keep you out of the hospital.

As for carats, they are units of measurement principally related to the physical weight of diamonds and gemstones. Now, if you are a person who has a voracious appetite for gemstones and diamonds, you must resist the craving to incorporate the carats into your diet by ingesting them. If you, for example, intentionally wolf down an expensive diamond-studded wedding ring, you will be whisked off to the nearest hospital to face an extended stay, very possibly in a psychiatric ward. So, if possible, chew carrots and eschew carats.

Question: Is it true that sugar daddies have a short life expectancy?

Answer: Based on my own exhaustive research, I would say that sugar daddies place themselves at considerable risk, as they are wont to do when they are elderly men, by consorting with much younger women, often referred to as hussies. A preponderance of these women are mercenaries who seek a sordid advantage over affluent elderly men who are likely to be physically and mentally vulnerable. These men often need professional caregivers and good friends to protect them from such temptresses.

Very fortunately, my Uncle Heimlich, who lived to the ripe old age of 104, was never victimized in this crass manner. He met Hilda in a gambling casino on his eighty-fifth birthday and four days later they married on her 24th birthday. When they moved to his mansion on a mountaintop in the northeastern corner of Idaho, Uncle Heimlich took immediate charge of their daily routine. Hilda, a born-and-raised city girl who had never been on a farm before, began her chores on the first day by attempting to milk the pigs and gather up cows' eggs. Immediately, Heimlich maneuvered to assign her other, less vital, work. To make matters worse, Hilda did not know how to cook or prepare meals and one evening nearly set the mansion on fire by failing to keep the stove door closed. As for their sex life, they, from the very onset of their cohabitation of the mansion, slept in separate bedrooms because of Hilda's stentorian snoring and Heimlich's smelly feet. You see, he rarely washed his two pairs of socks which he wore to bed. One year later, on his eight-sixth birthday, Uncle Heimlich drove Hilda to a remote railway station, where they kissed for the first time, bade each other farewell, and parted once and for all. As soon as Uncle Heimlich set foot in his home, he made a phone call and hired a local woman to be his round-the-clock caregiver. He lived the rest of his elongated life a contented and brimful man. Readers may draw whatever conclusions they wish about my uncle and other elderly men, but I will always admire the way in which Uncle Heimlich outmaneuvered my youthful step-grandmother, Hilda, who is now eighty-four and, I've recently learned, is married to a thirty-four-year-old bunco artist.

Question: Do calves have calves?

Answer: Yes. If you look toward the lower rear of their legs, you will see them just above their immature hooflets. Of course, if they ever have the notion of birthing calves themselves – an entirely different matter – they will have to wait until their mother cows give them consent to show off their alluring calves to a handsome bull.

Question: Do you, by any chance, enjoy classical music? If so, which composers are your favorites?

Answer: I will respond to your question by sharing a few playful anecdotes about some of my favorite composers.

Mr. Ferde Grofe'
Prepared his favorite souffle,'
Which he bent over to survey.
To his dismay,
In fell his toupee.
Tasting it, he liked it better that way.
Which saved the day.

The Mormon Tabernacle Choir
Cooked a giant fryer.
They turned up the fire,
Higher and higher.
Then to bed they did retire.
When they returned, they found a nasty pyre.

Mrs. Franz Liszt
Served her husband tasteless grist.
He left home in a huff, calling it a vile mess
Leaving Mrs. Liszt Lisztless

The Giacomo Puccinis
Served their guest just teeny zucchinis
To their delight,
The guest had little appetite.
Yet he thought the Puccinis
Untrustworthy meanies.

Mr. Anton Dvorak,
Cooking a very light flapjack
Flipped it far above his head.
He looked up with a frown,
For the morsel to come down.
After five days, he ate cornflakes instead.

Tomaso Albinoni
lunched upon an abalone.
The fish, an obvious phony, was much too bony.
So, at the advice of his musical crony,
Angelo Corelli,
He ate only the boneless belly.

Young Arturo Toscanini
Thought the veal scallopini
Too tough for his palate
So, for six hours each day,
Until he became gray
He hit it with a mallet.

Many years back
Mrs. J.B. Bach
Baked a muffin
Upon her oven.
Seeing the muffin bake,
The oven, a thief did take.
Mrs. Bach screamed in great shock,
"Bring my Offenbach."

Virtuoso Arthur Rubinstein,
Preparing to dine,
First savored a barcarolle.
He covered it with butter
Which makes one shudder,
To think of all that cholesterol.

Rimsky-Korsakov
Came down with the whooping cough.
The doctor prescribed broth.
His wife gave him chowder,
Which only made poor Rimsky Kov
Even louder.

Moe and Bea together made a birthday cake.
Moe would decorate, Bea would bake.
The cake turned into an ugly tart.
Perhaps it was Bea's oven, or Moe's art?

Mrs. Rachmaninoff
Served her husband beef stroganoff
With very little relish
She left off the sauce,
Which caused him remorse
So, he asked her to please embellish.

Mr. Gustav Mahler
Left the ice cream parlor
Quite hot under his collar
With one dollar he tried to pay
For a delicious sundae.
The sundae cost a dollar and a penny,
Just one penny too many,
Causing poor Gustav great woes
Over the debt he Berlioz.

Speaking of food and composers, I have it on good authority that Johannes Brahms had one day invited longtime friends for a dinner that largely consisted of his favorite noodle dishes. After dinner he and his friends set out to thoroughly dispose of the leftover noodles.

Without realizing it, they had left behind in a crevice of one of the pots two intertwined noodles. That evening the two noodles, in the privacy of the crevice, canoodled with rapture. In the morning, Brahms was astonished to find oodles of newborn noodles strewn about.

Regarding another well-known composer, oddly, it is a little-known historical fact that Franz Schubert invariably used his hollowed-out baton to slurp cherry sherberts after conducting orchestra performances. Yes, this was the obscure case of Schubert slurping sherberts.

Speaking of foods, I must confess to my readers that I am a terrible cook. Fortunately, I have a steadfast friend by the name of Mike Crowave who heats up delicious dinners for me each evening without craving praise or the slightest appreciation from me in return for his devotion.

Question: What do aunts and ants have in common?

Answer: Quite a bit, if the aunts keep an unkempt house.

Question: What causes the moon to shine so brightly on some nights?

Answer: Those are the nights that the Man in the moon serves many gallons of moonshine to the moon's inhabitants.

Question: Why do giraffes have such long necks?

Answer: It's because their heads are so very far from their shoulders.

Question: What is the difference between a mannequin and a dummy?

Answer: Mannequins, which are usually made from fiberglass or plastic, are placed in store windows, wearing attractive clothes. A dummy is a person who sends love letters to mannequins.

Question: How and why did the Lone Ranger
become the Lone Ranger?

Answer: His refusal to bathe and brush his teeth
(which is why he always wore a mask, mandated
by each town he visited) alienated practically
everyone but his horse, Silver, who always
managed to face straightaway from him as they
raced across the prairie. On the other hand,
governors of many prairie states – mostly men
who were strict constitutionalists and scholars on
matters related to public health, were also avowed
admirers of the Lone Ranger. For this reason,
they publicly and fiercely defended the masked
man with the argument that he needed no mask
because his personal hygiene was constitutionally
and strictly protected from all constraints imposed
by government.

Nevertheless, the Lone Ranger decided to wear
his mask voluntarily so that those of his
acquaintance could better bear the stench of his
oral fetidness. Many years later, the Lone Ranger
was saddened to discover that the words kemo
sabe – words Tonto used in addressing the Lone
Ranger – meant "Man with Malodorous Mouth."

Question: You haven't yet mentioned dentists. Is there anything you'd care to say about them?

One morning a neighborhood dentist, Dr. Molar, lost his wallet. He was in a frenzy because the wallet held a large wad of money as well as important credit cards and his license. On the morning Dr. Molar lost his wallet he was jogging on a hilly road. He returned to the road and scoured it with his eyes in search of the wallet but came home empty-handed. Not knowing what else to do, he decided to go to work in order to take his mind off his plight. He hid his emotions from his patients but evidently, they had detected that something was amiss in his manner and tone of speech. When he abruptly and tacitly left the office in the late afternoon, several patients and staff put their heads together in order to analyze and explain Dr. Molar's state of mind. What did they conclude?

They consensually acknowledged that Dr. Molar had been visibly and depressively down-in-the-mouth that afternoon while attending to his patients.

Question: Are frogs harmful to human beings?

Answer: Generally, no. However, at times they can be quite alarming, as for example, the time when a passenger aboard a Delta flight discovered a frog in his underwear, frantically seeking egress while the Fasten Your Seat Belt sign was lighted, prohibiting passengers to get up to take care of such urgent matters.

Question: Is it true that giraffes have three hearts? If it is true, how does it affect their behavior?

Answer: Yes, giraffes do have three hearts and that unusual characteristic markedly shapes their dating and mating propensities, since it is rare that all three hearts will throb for the same mate. So, if you study giraffeology carefully (as I have), you will learn that each giraffe will simultaneously fall in love with as many as three other giraffes, all with their multiple hearts. Another oddity to note is their aversion to necking during their courtships, evidently because this romantic enterprise would take them an inordinate amount of time to reach erotic fulfillment.

Question: Why is it that the general public hears very little about termites except in exterminator ads?

Answer: Because they are interminably boring.

Question: What is the difference between a psychiatrist and a psychologist?

Answer: Usually about twenty dollars.

Question: What do typhoons and tycoons have in common?

Answer: Both are usually offensive blowhards.

Question: What is the difference between a snort and snot?

Answer: Firstly, the word snort has the letter r, and the word snot does snot. Secondly, a snort usually serves the worthy purpose of draining snot. Snot, on the other hand, often serves the unworthy purpose of spoiling a romantic moment.

Question: Do you know the precise meaning of the words hors d'oeuvre?

Answer: An hors d'oeuvre, as you probably know, is a small savory dish served as a kind of appetizer.

Question: Well, what then, is a horse d'oeuvre?

Answer: A horse d'oeuvre, as you probably don't know, is a small mound of alfalfa hay with a topping of sliced fruit and carrots.

Question: What is the most effective way to break a person from the habit of chain smoking?

Answer: It's quite simple: Just take their chains away from them.

Question: What is unique about the milkweed plant?

Answer: It is the only known plant that sprouts udders with which they suckle their younglings.

Question: What is a blitzkrieg?

Answer: "Blitz" in German means "lightning" and "Krieg" in the same language means squabble or conflict. In other words, a "blitzkrieg" is from start to finish a short war that ends decisively.

Readers might also wish to know a few things about the word "blintzekrieg." A blintzekrieg is a squabble that usually takes place in the kitchen of a Jewish family. The women of the family – Momma, her daughter(s), grandma and Aunt Sadie (almost all Jewish families have an Aunt Sadie) repeatedly squabble over who makes the most exquisitely delicious blintzes. As always, there are no winners or losers of this argument and afterward everyone is entirely agreeable until they find another subject to bicker about.

Question: What can you tell your readers about fleas?

Reply: There was once a flea that alit upon a sheep. Finding nothing there that he could gulp down, he burrowed into the wool of the sheep until he found a nice, warm, cushiony surface. As soon as he began to nibble on the skin of the sheep he was assaulted by large, foul-smelling and ferocious teeth that came gnashing at his tiny, defenseless body. With one gigantic leap he vaulted out of his snare onto the ground and sped away to safety. This spectacular feat is now known as the unique case of the Flea Fleeing Fleece.

Question: What was your most interesting experience with a member of the animal kingdom?

Answer: One day when I was driving my dog to her veterinarian, I saw a goose walking with six of her goslings, one behind the other. Out of the corner of my eye I noticed that the goslings were aligned in a straight row alongside their mother. However, every so often one or more of them would veer toward a few of the parked cars on the street. Each time they did, the mother would intercept it, causing both to dangerously bang against a car or two. The mother's fear and frustration were visibly mounting. When I pulled into the vet's driveway, I was astonished to discover that the mother goose and her goslings had followed me right up to the doorway.

The veterinarian, as it happened, had viewed this entire scenario from the front door with evident concern and bemusement. Next, he found a way to corral the goslings and their mother into the building. He then yelled to me that he was going to examine the goose and then take them back to the county park whence they had come. After carrying out these tasks, he and I sat down for a chat. I asked the vet for his assessment of the goose he had examined. He said that she had just had the harrowing experience of protecting her offspring from recurrent danger and needed a bit of time to recover. I asked the vet if there happened to be a formal medical diagnosis that would shed light on her condition. He said there was such a diagnosis: she suffered from a mild case of goose pimples.

I humbly submit this stirring story to the reader as one of the many Mother Goose fables that have been written over the centuries.

Question: Are there any medical practices of which you disapprove and, if so, why?

Answer: Personally, I think it is shocking that nurses and doctors are allowed to take their patients' blood pressure. To think they have the right to remove their patients' blood pressure and then leave them to soldier through such an experience on their own is certainly unforgiveable medical misconduct.

I do appreciate, however, the good work of phlebotomists, who draw and prepare small amounts of blood for medical testing, transfusions or donation. In my conversations with phlebotomists, I have learned that some are excellent musicians who play their phlebot in local orchestras.

Question: What is your favorite nursery rhyme?

Answer: My favorite nursery rhyme begins with the words, "Mary had a little lamb, and all the local obstetricians were astonished. And everywhere that Mary went, the docs were sure to go." Another of my favorite nursery rhymes goes as follows: "Jack be nimble, Jack be quick. Jack jumped over the candlestick and burnt his tuchis."

Question: Are you by any chance a sports enthusiast?

Answer: Yes, I am and thanks for asking. In my youth I played on my high school basketball team and "ran" track, breaking the contemporaneous record for the four-hour mile. Afterward, I took up the sport of tennis in which I excelled by playing exclusively against men who were certifiably at least thirty-nine years older than myself. Now I am a spectator of major sports and entertain myself by learning and memorizing the record-breaking achievements of our greatest athletes.

The most spectacular and memorable of all records was, in my estimation, the record set by Harry Bagwell in 1889. Harry Bagwell was the equipment manager and chief of the grounds crew for the Chicago White Stockings. In that capacity, he had the privilege of possessing a key to the equipment room. Each night, when the stadium had emptied, he would sneak into this room and poach ten or fifteen bases that had been stored there. By the end of the season, he had stolen a total of three hundred and seventy-two bases, far surpassing the record of Hugh Nicol, a baseball star who stole 138 bases in 1887 for the Chicago White Stockings (look it up).

Harry Bagwell sold the bases on the black market for twenty dollars apiece, so he came away with contraband worth almost $3,000. Sadly, it was not long before Harry Bagwell was arrested for his crimes and sentenced to six years in a state prison. The sentence was then commuted to four years when he agreed to a judge's ruling that he change his name from Bagwell to Bag of Slops, a name that will live in infamy in our baseball annals for all time.

Question: Are you fond of birds and, if so, what bird is your favorite?

Answer: I am fond of birds, but my favorite is the ooh-ooh-ow-ow bird of Hawaii. This bird lays square eggs and each time it does, it screams "Ooh-ooh, ow-ow."

A bird that is not entitled to my fondness is the stork. The legendary stork has been delivering babies to expectant parents for centuries. From my own vantage point, I believe the storks' deliveries are as frequent and abundant as Amazon's, both on an international and domestic scale. This ornithological recklessness has undoubtedly contributed to population explosions and famine throughout the world.

Question: Have you heard of the fabled tale of the inseparable friendship between the herring and the whale?

Answer: Yes, I have. One day a school of fish found the herring without his friend the whale. They swam up to the herring and anxiously asked, "Where is your friend, the whale?" He replied, "How should I know, am I my blubber's kipper?

Question: What is the handiest way to recollect how many days are in each month?

Answer: In 1425 someone wrote the following: "Thirty days hath September," a traditional verse used to remember how many days were in each month of the calendar year. It goes as follows:

"Thirty days hath September, April, June, and November.

All the rest have thirty-one.

February has twenty-eight but leap year coming one in four,

February then has one day more."

I have always considered this verse to be a dandy way to remember the number of days of each month. However, I have recently decided to replace this verse with one of my own in order to ease the stress of readers. So, instead, try this verse on for size.

"Thirty days has Septober,

April, May and no wonder,

All except for my grandmother,

And she walked to work."

I certainly hope you are enriched by this substitution.

Question: What would you say is the most valuable usage of a shoehorn?

Answer: I would say that the most valuable usage of a shoehorn is when it blares a very loud noise just as someone steps on your foot.

Question: What is the difference between a stalactite and a stalagmite?

Answer: A stalactite has three tees, and a stalagmite has only two tees.

Question: I have had trouble sleeping at night. What would you recommend?

Answer: The key to a restful sleep is, I contend, a down pillow. I never miss a chance to recommend down pillows to my friends and, by the way, even to stray pedestrians on crowded street corners as well. I tell them that if they are genuinely questing for an uplift in the quality of their lives, they should definitely find a way to get themselves down.

Question: Does such a monster as the Devil really exist?

Answer: Reliable polls have consistently indicated that a small majority of Americans do indeed believe in the Devil. It seems that the more religious the person, the more likely she or he will believe in his existence. My own research has uncovered several obscure, albeit authentic documents in an unrenowned library that seem to confirm the fact that the Devil is omnipresent among us.

In his own hand, the Devil has provided accounts of his secretive visits to the executive conference rooms of America's petroleum industry over the course of many decades. He describes how he each time transformed himself into the coatrack that stood, unnoticed, in a corner of the room. There he carefully listened in on the discussions of these giants of industry as they largely conversed about monetary matters such as how to maximize the company's profits with clever innovations, while the Devil furtively took notes on a small pad.

Every so often, someone in the group, a knowledgeable maverick no doubt, would interrupt the discussion with a question having to do with the potential of extracted and refined oil to contaminate the environment, overheat the seas and cause general climatic havoc. The men politely listened and then went on with their palaver, never heeding the words spoken by the maverick. This pattern, according to the Devil's notes, was repeated many times over.

The Devil then decided to visit state legislatures, mostly in the South. Again, he disguised himself as a coatrack. He listened carefully and took notes. He was thrilled to hear legislators champion laws to suppress the voting rights of citizens of color as well as women's reproductive rights but was especially uplifted by the indifference of the corporations he had earlier visited to the cataclysmic horrors of climate change.

The Devil took his notes home with him while chuckling along the way over how he could now take unwinding vacations from his nefarious work since human institutions were carrying out his worldwide mission far more adeptly and diabolically than he could ever attain himself.

The Devil had some of his notes transcribed and bound in a volume that is squirreled away in an obscure library. In an ebullient frenzy of joy, he chewed into small pieces and swallowed his more detailed notes, perhaps unknowingly inspiring a new adage: THE DETAILS ARE IN THE DEVIL.

About the Author

Gerald Amada, Ph.D. is the author of thirteen books in four genres: fiction, humor, psychotherapy, and college student conduct issues. He has been a guest lecturer at over 150 colleges and universities throughout the United States and Canada and has authored over seventy articles and book reviews in professional journals. He was the Director the City College of San Francisco Mental Health Program and maintained a private psychotherapy practice in Marin County, California, both for about thirty years.

For more information about Dr. Amada, and links to his published works, please see his website at: http://geraldamada.com/